undressed and unbridled beat poetry

by elliot m rubin

Library of Congress
Copyright November 2024
ISBN   979-8-9922464-5-2
E-Book 979-8-9922464-6-9

Library of Congress Control Number 2025903505

    No part of this book may be reproduced in any form whatsoever without the author's prior express written consent.
    This book is fiction, and all names, people, places, and happenings are from the author's imagination and are used fictionally.
    Any resemblance to living or dead persons and/or businesses, locations, or events is entirely coincidental.
    All rights reserved

Published 2025
elliot m rubin
Monroe Township N.J.

Preface

I believe poetry is to be read and understood by all, and it needs to be written, for the most part, in plain language for everyone's enjoyment.

Too often, poets write in-depth, penetrating poems where you need to be well-read and/or versed in literary minutia to appreciate the poetry, not this book or any of my writings. I try to write so everyone can enjoy a few moments of intellectual satisfaction without consulting a dictionary or encyclopedia all the time.

Disclaimer

This book of poetry is **not intended** to be read by prudes, political book-banning conservatives, and/or sexually inhibited and repressed small-minded dolts.

Dedication

To my grandchildren
Shane, Isabelle, Jonathan, Carter,
Alexandra, Melanie, Mollie, and Madison

In memory of my father

Herman S. Rubin
who wrote poetry, prayers, and letters all his life

What is Progressive Beat Poetry

Progressive beat poetry is a type of poetry that goes against the usual rules and traditions. It discusses social, political, and cultural issues to make people more aware and push for change. Here are some key points about progressive poetry:

- **Questioning the Norms**: Progressive beat poets often challenge and question the main social, political, and cultural ideas of society. They dive into complex topics like race, gender, and power.
- **Voices and Inclusion**: This poetry style aims to give a voice to those who are often ignored. It highlights stories and experiences that don't usually get attention.
- **Thinking and Talking**: Progressive beat poetry makes readers think about more significant societal issues and encourages meaningful conversations. It aims to start discussions and inspire actions towards social justice.
- **Breaking the Mold**: Progressive poets often play with form and structure, moving away from traditional styles to express their messages better.

Progressive beat poetry seeks to break free from traditional poetic conventions and push the boundaries of language, space-as-art, and expression.

Table of Contents

- NAKED NATION 9
- ELOISE 10
- PRIESTESS 11
- I AM NOT NUTS 12
- FUNERAL 13
- SURPRISE LETTER 14
- GIRLS OF THE NIGHT 15
- TAXI TAXI 16
- MANHATTAN 17
- DRIVE-TIME 18
- CROSS COUNTRY TRIP 19
- LAUNDRY 20
- COFFEE 1964 21
- SEEDS 22
- TOMORROW 23
- GOING HOME 24
- NEW YORK YANKEES 25
- IN NEED 26
- BEDROOMS 27
- ADULTHOOD 28
- AT THE DISPENSARY 29
- FALLEN ANGEL 30
- MIRRORS 31
- JERSEY DINERS 32
- GENERATION Z 33
- VENUS FLYTRAP 34
- 2024 ELECTION 35
- FALL IS ENDING 36
- DONUT HEAVEN 37
- SHE 38
- LONER 39
- FINALITY 40
- WEEKEND RETREAT 41
- GOLDEN CALIFORNIA 42
- VANISHED 43
- LATKE TALK ABOUT 44
- FINE DINING 45
- MARRIAGE BLISS 46
- WHOLEEE SPIRIT 47

LONE OAK TREE	48
MAY-DECEMBER MARRIAGE	49
RELIGIOUS SCHOOL GIRL	50
RETURN TO SENDER	51
AFTERNOON IN PARADISE	52
PENS	53
CASINO ON CHRISTMAS EVE	54
THANKSGIVING DINNER	55
MEMORY OF YOUTH	56
CHEESEBURGER	58
DOCTOR DOCTOR	59
DRONES IN NEW YORK	60
BLACK PEARL	61
BE THE TORNADO	62
JUST ANOTHER SCHOOL SHOOTING	63
BREAKUP	64
FULL CIRCLE	65
URBAN FARMETTE	66
EYES OF LOVE	67
I DON'T HAVE ANSWERS	68
CHRISTMAS EVE	69
FISH EYES	70
JOLLY OLD LONDON	71
EARLY MORNING DRAMA	72
RESURRECTION	73
REALITY OF LIFE	74
HEART FLUTTERS	75
BRIAN SICKNICK	76
MAY-DECEMBER	77
FOOD FOR THOUGHT	78
HONESTY	79
RIDING THROUGH MANHATTAN	80
HER RAT CITY	81
FIVE SENSES	82
AUGUST 31ST	83
TEARS FOR DEMOCRACY	84
MISSING	85
LIBRARY PICKUP	86
FIVE	87
AT SEVENTEEN	88
POETRY IS POWER	89

SMILE	90
RECIPE FOR CAKE	91
RELATIONSHIP	92
INSPIRATION	93
LOST LOVE	94
JOAN 1953	95
MANHATTAN STREETS	96
SEARCHING	97
SMALL LOSSES	98
LOSS	99
MISTER RIGHT NOW	100
SUPERMARKET PARKING LOT	101
WHOSE SIDE IS GOD ON IN WAR	102
LONER	103
OBSERVER	104
MOTHER ACORN	105
PAIN	106
TEA SANDWICHES	107
CITY LIVING	108
STUFF	109
FOX HUNTING	110
BRONX METAPHORS	111
UNNAMED WOMAN	112
MIRAGE	113
LOVING HUSBAND	114
THEY SAID TO ME	115

naked nation

lady liberty's laid bare
   undressed and naked
her virtues negated
   oligarchs stampede
across national morals
   liberty, fraternity, equality
stomped upon and crushed
   under billionaire greed
for power, financial gain, not need
   innocence oppressed
by high prices, low growth
   while the rich suckle
on the teats of the working class
   elected whores in congress
collect high salaries,
   fully paid, better health care, and
a pension for life after serving a term
   money donations into election campaigns
to enslave and ensure the prostitute vote
   for their political donor's best interests
ignoring a nation's welfare and well-being

eloise

she is his muse and lover
of slight build, thin,
short brunette hair in a pixie cut,
her looks average, a
ballerina in youth
every movement of her body
a sensual artistic declaration
of love and availability
captures inspiration
and emotional creativity
until the day she leaves

nothing he did or didn't do,
a child of the 60s' free love lifestyle
her unshaven body attracts lovers
like honey to bears, irresistible to many,
one day, she poses with another model
and instantly attracts her romantic advances

he is crushed, confused, inconsolable
she tried to leave for vacation, an excuse
to not make it worse, but her libido
denied her patience, she left with a kiss
promising to return in a month
intending to be with
her new lover forever
but forever for her
is till the next infatuation arrives

priestess

she fell from grace and led a life of sinful lust
found redemption in the church of eighty-proof
with a congregation of fellow sinners every night
reached out to the needy in the holy shrine of liquor
in a tavern on the back road out of town

only preachers lay hands on her as they pray
on her divine temple located at the clitoral altar
of wanton urges and cry out for god continually
during a sermon of passion for restoration
of their soul with her willing holy spirit and body

in a backwoods motel room, services are held
king-size prayer sheets soiled with sinners' seed
collection plate on the dresser always filled
donations every time they pray with her
then go home again as leaders of community

i am not nuts
"I am out with lanterns, looking for myself"— Emily Dickinson (1855)

my hour is up
                                        no
i did not find myself today
                            not here, though
the doctor suggested a med
                          nothing with my head
i'd been looking in high proofs
                          met a lot of friends there
yet couldn't end my search
                          blackout love left me empty
i do remember hangovers
                          headaches cured with more
devil-rum now felt bored
                            its entreaties fell short
when i awoke
                                  someplace
unknown
                                    undressed
bruised
                                      abused
hospitalized
                                      pregnant
alone with my thoughts
                                  and body aches

i finally found myself

funeral

a funeral parlor is located next door
black luxury cars line up down the block
tissues and handkerchiefs point out grievers
the stately building is a stopover in life
next is a final resting place
as a cherrywood casket with brass accents
wheels out to the glossily waxed hearse
mourners stand aside and watch in silence

the beloved is shoved into the back, slid in, secured,
before the vehicle slowly leaves for the cemetery,
where the dirt mound, next to a six-foot hole, where
a graveside service awaits   and angels stand aside

waiting

to bring bastard bernard to his reward, although he
was never a believer; the dead have no vote or voice
in their final arrangements, and earlier, satan
grabbed his soul because debts need to be repaid

surprise letter

the years we spent together
were filled with love;
vacationed everywhere
until her unexpected fatality
by an eighteen-wheel truck
devastated my life
left behind beautiful memories —
i loved her completely
never questioned her goings, comings, friendliness;
always greeted me with smiles, hugs, kisses;
then, one day, a letter arrived —
it's twenty years since she passed
now, a young woman wrote
about a DNA test
enclosed pictures of herself hugging my wife
we had no children

unbeknownst to me
my wife was her mum, and i,
due to the test, am her father;
seems she had another family
where her company had a satellite office
she visited a week at a time, then
disappeared with her death, now
her secret life bounces from the letter,
rips my heart open,
to release depression and bewilderment
this explains why, years ago, she
wore extremely loose clothes
with no answers   except she's gained weight

girls of the night

i see them in the city
on side street corners
under unbecoming glare
of the halogen lamp's
pure white light
dressed in skimpy outfits
their goods for sale exposed

some are beautiful, tall, and thin
some not,
everyone has their kinks
yet none are ugly to all
they're someone's daughter
or lover
and they sell themselves often

pleasure bought in minutes
no place sacred
doorways become marital beds
next is not limited to the deli counter

these girls have hidden feelings
behind a tough facade
because their life
is often placed in danger
by abusive men who appear kind
until behind closed doors

taxi taxi

sixth avenue
midtown manhattan
swirls with traffic
yellow cabs swerve left, right
pick up passengers
unlicensed car service
cuts a taxi off, both stop,
shout at each other in tongues

police arrive, followed by
ambulance's sirens scream
people gawk
pickpockets slither among them
lift wallets
handoff to accomplices

working girls move
from crowded sidewalk
to eighth avenue
cruise curbs
flash bare skin to attract buyers
who cut off cabs, trucks
to swing recklessly across traffic
in attempts to purchase

manhattan

an island
full of idiosyncratic people
some just idiotic
lustful, luring streets
with entreaties from sweeties
luckily, i only visit
like millions do
avoid tourist traps
too expensive
too many
   work here
   live there
survival imperative
a unique city
in a nation of turbulence

drive-time

my car is moving
early morning drive-time
the expressway packed tight
heading to the verrazanno
to brooklyn
a daydream memory entices
i'm back in northern boulder, colorado
eating certified prime beef
a thick, tasty, medium cooked
buttered rib-eye steak
au-jus fills the plate
most delicious one i ever ate
i'd go back tomorrow if i could
just to have another meal;
then my car
pulls onto the driveway at work
i have no recollection
of driving there
    and now i'm hungry

cross country trip

as a high school teenager
my college-aged neighbor
drove cross country
i so wanted to do it, too

in my sixties, i started to plan
bought a book on how to drive it
read northern and southern routes
and where to sightsee everywhere

my younger friend richard just retired
we were going to do it together someday
the talks and discussions were fun
then richard was in a bike accident

he died with everything to live for
now seventy-nine i regret waiting
my dream of driving to california
passed with richard, plus i lost the book

laundry

when you run out of clean
did you ever throw everything
in the wash
to watch them tumble dry
then peer intently
through a round glass window
and think this is symbolic
of society's troubles
or the last tumbles
in your bedsheets
intertwined with someone
who, when the cycle is over,
and all dried out and relaxed
leaves the laundry room, finished,
not to return for weeks
if ever

coffee 1964

i sat in a small diner in manhattan
after my college speed reading class
black coffee served in a white mug —
back then, other than licorice,
it was the only black my lips could touch —
in my brooklyn high school
daisy sat in my economics class
we would talk often at lunch
she'd sit at the table behind mine —
on the cafeteria food line
we flirted, smiled, and often
both of us complained about school food —
once
she placed her hand on my arm
as we laughed about something;
i don't remember what it was, but
her face still haunts me
nothing more happened
and i liked her —
sixty years later
melanin still segregates
too many of today's politicians
continue to drink their coffee
in lily white mugs

seeds

a farmer's field
blazed yellow
as sunflowers
embarrassed the sun
too tall   too bright
ants wallow below
          in shade
too tired to climb
they settle for fallen seeds
like russian peasants do
for bread crumbs
while oligarchs sail away
in fabulous yachts
bought
with blood-soaked money
they stole from masses
while moscow's mothers
desperately
look for sons
who died in ukraine
for putin's folly
to suckle them again
held tight
but never will
          or even bury them

tomorrow

kangaroos will still hop
every morning
the sun will still be here
desire flourishes with hope
love burns bright
    till extinguished
it doesn't matter
    what god wants
mankind's imbued
    with self-determination
the world rotates
    despite a deity
the universe as we know it
    pays homage
to the god of physics
the lord of chaos
while children commit suicide
as others dip cookies in milk
tomorrow
kangaroos will still hop

going home

once you leave the nest
trees grow, limbs break off, trunks cut
a forest might look static, but
time changes things
similar yet different
after fifty-seven years
the block i grew up on is still there
homes repainted different colors
lawns and landscaping changed
some homes now have gates
everything looks familiar
everything looks different
most of my childhood buddies died
most of them scattered like dust in the wind
at night
i see everyone again
as my eyes drift off to sleep
my secure world lives on
in memory
forever

new york yankees

three of us subwayed to the bronx
to see a ballgame at the stadium
the urine-stenched train
shakes side to side on aged tracks
as a blind accordion player
walks from one car to the next
without falling between them
while bellows blast out tunes
as his fingers run up and down a keyboard
faster than base runners stealing home plate
yet he never bumps into a pole
and that day, yogi pinch-hit a single,
whitey pitched, but mickey didn't homer,
though my buddies hoped he did
but i a brooklyn dodger fan,
knew how to get to ebbets field by bus
and in 1955 rooted wildly
when they won the world series
as i was walking home past flatbush avenue
car horns blared, people shouted from windows
the borough cheered, and everyone was ecstatic
october in brooklyn became times square
on new year's eve when the ball drops —
i played hooky the next day with my pals
we replayed every inning of the game,
but two years later, my heart broke,
when my beloved dodgers struck out
for tinsel-town   and crushed a young boy's heart

in need

with a teenage daughter
adrift
no skill other than her body
no alimony
since he is in another country
money's tight
rent due
no steady boyfriend
yet tall, thin, blond, and
in her early forties
sexually liberated
she becomes a pole dancer
works for tips

nudity doesn't faze her
tries to make a few dollars
while still asking friends for cash
said she would only dance
and not do things men want
at a gentlemen's club
unless she is off work
on a date
      for free
although other girls
engage and engorge
in a private v.i.p. club room
to make ends meet, literally

bedrooms

their rooms are different
yet all similar
located nationwide
they're all museums
frozen in time
nothing has been moved
pajamas strewn
dolls and toys left in place
favorite hoodies unwashed
library books decades unreturned
and nearby
in a cemetery
    are the children
    who left for school
in congress
    are the politicians
    who voted
to allow school shootings
by their inaction to prevent them

adulthood

instructions say open here
but life doesn't come with them
once you leave home
you're on your own
forever

what to do for a career
who to date, boys or girls
do you want kids
decisions, decisions,
there are too many

being grown up is not all that great
easier to play house when you're young
with no parents around to solve life's problems
they can fester
until you find solutions

adulthood is not all wine and roses
sometimes, we indulge in too much vino
the sweet florals never last too long
unexpectedly, lightning strikes,
then we die

at the dispensary

there is no line
which is unusual
considering there's a sale
forty percent off is a big discount
on wacky weed products
since it became legal

the counter girl has
many requisite tattoos
rising up her arms, and
even sides of fingers
while her sweatshirt
appears rather tight
she wears it as a bodysuit
when her head turns
unkempt blond hair
   flags in the air
she's sweet
and helpful
and a reader
and a poet

i give her my card
she asks me to recite
one of my pieces
which i do; it touches her soul
because a tear appears —
angels are everywhere
when a spoken word touches them

fallen angel

i'm waiting right here
where is the love you shared —
those moments live on
not buried or forgotten
didn't you care
my broken heart misses
the warmth you gave me
with a loving, tender kiss
something i'll truly miss
wish you were with me again
don't you care
was i a throwaway spare
my bed is made,
waiting for you
sheets ironed, wrinkle-free
since you made creases in my life
i need you back to smooth them out
your letter on the dresser
said it's goodbye forever
why is my heart's painful cry
although we only met last night
i thought we had something right
your walking out is a heartbreak sight
don't you care

mirrors

when we look in a mirror
we either see
what we want to see
or a disturbing truth

does reality strike us gently
a feather's touch on a cheek
or the proverbial punch in the nose
mirrors don't lie, honest brokers

they're middlemen in life's march
soldiers sent into combat
going forward with no choice
to face what is ahead

the silvered glass reflects
a lover's face after a kiss
or the sadness of a final goodbye
before we walk away   forever

jersey diners

acclaimed nationwide
the diner's dinners are known for variety
menus two feet tall, fully food-filled
what to have, what to order

sunday's soup is cream of broccoli
monday beef vegetable
tuesday mushroom barley
wednesday chicken orzo
thursday split pea with croutons
friday manhattan clam chowder
saturday's soup is cream of mushroom

if you can name it, you can order it
the wide range of meals is astounding
plus, the jersey attitude of waitresses
adds just the right amount of spice

generation z

she decided to leave
at morning light
the evening before
was a fun time
bar drinks, group singing
when eyes met in the crowd
unexplained electricity
i never experienced before
our conversation easy
my feelings for her fireworks
she's a hot pepper i gladly devoured
and after a few light kisses   we left

i don't like to talk about happenings
but we had a good time that night
we made plans to meet up again

    soon

but her phone number didn't work
it was to an old age nursing home
and the woman who answered
with her name was in her nineties

i felt used and cheap

venus flytrap

its petals look soft
the stamen desired
its nectar attracts
once a victim touches,
its jaws close and trap
then devours its captive
as in local dance clubs
where women dress
in provocative clothes
breasts barely covered
they attract their suitors
with a smile and a scent
once a drink is bought
the game begins to end
an unsuspecting man
believes it's first-sight love
and the honey trap is set
a life of romance expected
until bank accounts drained

2024 election

let's turn the page,
she said,
not enough people listened
they went backward
instead of forward

we all were here before
when hundreds of thousands died
of disease
due to incompetence
now it seems
life is on a loop
the past is in the future

chaos and ignorance rule

fall is ending

as morning dew freezes
it crunches underfoot
crossing the lawn
as he leaves
and the warmth of home
becomes a memory
while squirrels race under bushes
to chase each other
in a frenzied dash
with bird's nests
exposed high in the trees
strong winds
sweep the last red leaves
off branches to fly about
then land and decompose
to become dust
slowly on the ground
no longer the green, solid leaf,
the love of a wife
suddenly exposed
to a wildly wandering husband
who neglects family
for carnal moments
with a younger woman,
who sees an easy street in life
with an older man
and ignores the damage done
to innocents

donut heaven

i didn't realize the opportunity
a donut shop would have for me
until i tried a chocolate crème
a filled round one with dark chocolate
overwhelming the top, as my taste buds
exploded in orgasmic ecstasy

the franchise booklet looked delicious
my salivary glands sealed the deal
i bought the shop and set it up
donut heaven for non-diabetics
every flavor on display behind glass
where skinny folks grow a juicy fat ass

cinnamon holes and powdered sugar
vanilla cream or chocolate-filled
if you eat one, remember
i sell it fresh and hot
buy a donut or a dozen lot
leave your diet at the door
eat one, and you'll want twelve more

she

caused my first heartbreak
at sixteen, hormones raged
the result of a girl's kiss
and a repeat when we meet

i remember her name
and where she lived
sixty plus years flew by
a first love   doesn't die

loner

a friendless child
no kids on the block
after school went home
did math and reading
never outside to play ball
from
sewer cover to sewer cover
with neighborhood children
not because of an infirmity
but it's a problem
living on a cul-de-sac
with only one street sewer

finality

yesterday
was my first time back
it's been six months
since dad died
the brown mound
was not seeded
below it
a plain wooden box
contains my beloved father
a brilliant mind silenced,
a person
who overflowed with empathy
as i stood silently
i whispered
i love you
hoping his spirit heard me
i don't believe in an afterlife
yet
here i was
as if it existed
wish i could logically explain

but death is always final

weekend retreat

the drive to the hotel
went fast
a swingers fest enticed me —
at the welcome dinner
i mingled and met someone
she invited me
to visit her room after we ate—
her long red hair
covers virgin pink nipples
as her body
star-fishes on the bed
straddle me, she implores
on our first date —
without hesitation, i undress
then reality sets in
how old are you
races from my mouth
future years in prison stop me
better angels march in my mind
she looks young
but the door bouncers check ages
celibate is better than cell bait
old enough,
i'm here with my parents,
and i'm legal

golden california

the sun's glare glistens
on the pacific
as a tanned
surfer girl washes in
her golden body taut
drips salt-water
while beaches
full of sun worshipers watch
her too-small bikini triangles
stretch over bountiful breasts
while her boyfriend watches
her walk to him
she dries off
exposing a california
laidback attitude

after both sunbathe
they leave to go home
graduation is tomorrow

today parents excited
for their futures
as students gather
to walk in the assembly
when a younger student
opens fire with an automatic rifle
ends fifteen young lives

vanished

i knew her for a year or two
she was an excellent poet
her poems were memoirs
wrote real-life times in rhymes

there were over one hundred
gathered together and edited
put into book form in date order
finally, her issues are to be in print

a publisher contact was made
soon, her book would be a reality
a contract was drawn and ready
then the poet disappeared, totally

wrote to her many times for naught
her social media was abandoned, too
phone calls were never answered
why did this giant talent disappear

latke talk about

they booked a cruise

to arugula island
in the caribbean
their clothes
were an art deco
parsley pattern with twirls
and they carrot
wait to see it
since their passports
had all the
peas and quesos
properly done

i knew
they could ketchup later
if we romaine
in the hotel
until they lettuce go to the beach
where i can see
a russian dressing
into a bikini

fine dining

the food is okay, waiters scurry about
kitchen door swings back and forth
trays of food brought out as i quietly sit
waiting for mine when this young woman enters
asks to join me for dinner

when i look at her, i feel like a winner, why did she
pick my table to eat, but she did ask if i was alone
thank you, i think i'll join you she said, although i
did not ask her

beautiful women can do this since my hollywood
contract never arrived; who's to ask why, i thought
with a sigh; my mission is to love and then die, plus
all the other tables are full, that's why

our conversation was great; as i ate, but nothing
came of it; you should know we finished, and then
said our goodbyes, as she left me with a heart full of
my sighs

marriage bliss

married twenty years
like other couples
problems arose
nothing insurmountable
he was in sports leagues at night
she joined afternoon sewing circles
housekeeping kept up
dusting, vacuuming, laundry

lipstick stains
on his tighty whities
led to a blowup
he yelled
i'm leaving you for miranda

she replied
go ahead,
and willie junior isn't yours

wholeee spirit

they elbow their way in
buy big bargains
things not needed

but low prices
consume emotions
empty wallets
bury the holy spirit

of a celebratory event
preachers preach about
then cast aside
when the revered word

sale is said
bank accounts empty
and loved one's love
is bought with gifts

then strewn
on the floor
      forgotten
          two weeks later

lone oak tree

i am old now
a tree with decades of growth rings
my branches sag
from too many life experiences

my friend's leaves
already dropped
the ground welcomes them
as they transform into mulch

though my roots are deep
disease and events weaken me
new-growth shoots branch out
and presently grow far away

when i fall
it will not be a gentle tumble
but one heard in the deaf forest

and the other trees will continue on

may-december marriage

he was not poor
a well-to-do middle class
elderly man
still lucid
with digestive issues
copied millionaire
john jacob astor

had a wet nurse
for nutrition
who was twenty-something

pert with flowing hair
inclusion in his will, her goal,
she overlooked
    the age difference
he died with all his teeth
lips frozen in a smile

religious school girl

early morning prayers
praise the lord
her plaid skirt below the knee
prevents boys having a see
later
when classes finish
her skirt rolls up at the waist
exposes virgin knock knees
to meet a bad boy at the corner
smoke a filtered fag and
chew forbidden gum
sneak in a hidden dark alley
hands roam till holy rome found
prayers said in throes of thanks
minutes of forbidden fruit tasted
later expelled from eden's garden
by an elderly woman who walking past
tries to shame teens in love
forgets years past when she was young
and had a mouth filled
with a bad boy's tongue

return to sender

on the highway to manhattan
a racist rode right in front
his car had shock stickers
curses about blacks,
puerto ricans, and non-english speakers

the biggest one was a maga
send'em back screed
kids born here to illegals
need to leave, too
but there's a big problem

seems a president's mother
jumped ship years ago,
and stayed
her son now has to leave
poor ireland gets to keep him

afternoon in paradise

they spoke often
many similarities
their first date is blind

she greets him and asks
can you help me
trim my moggy

afterward,
he brushes cut hair away
helps wash it in the shower

now soft and smooth
he gently pets it
'till it purrs and stirs

held it close to his face
kisses it
then puts it to bed

pens

i'm tired of fake caring
when doctors see you for minutes
your life in their pens
only to have insurance deny
hospitals kick you out
well or not

politicians
have law-based-medical pens
women die for lack of care
sick laws kill sick mothers to be
both fetus and carrier
fall off the cliff of cure

voters fail to use their pens
to check off
ignorant politicians
then wonder why
their moms, sisters, daughters
are canceled from living

casino on christmas eve

it's been years
since i celebrated christmas
as a youngster my home life
was worse than miserable
mom an alcoholic, dad rarely home
he caroused with booze and whores
while gifts bought in thrifts
were either too big or too small

i sought relief when older
in the arms of paid lovers
in emotionless encounters
till midnight mass passed
and left her in bed in the paid-for room

went downstairs to the casino
where i'd play at a card table
next to an overweight, wrinkly brunette
telling me her social security checks
start in january, the alcohol told me
she likes younger men
as another whisky sour
pours down her throat,
when her pile of chips grows higher,
she offers me a stack
to go back to her room
for a nightcap —
i took the chips, celebrated
in somebody's grandmother's bed

thanksgiving dinner

it's early afternoon
the family is all here
my
eight grandkids
four adult kids
two daughters-in-law
two nieces
one sister-in-law
one nephew and wife

while my wife cooks
the appetizers are set out
low hum of everyone echos
i sneak into the garage

quite

very quiet

open
a can of beer
stand there
in noiseless bliss

memory of youth

a young boy wanders
through a world he knows
past tall oak trees
with limbs stretched out
and green leaves aflutter

mr dowd's dog joins the stroll
stops at mrs collin's rose bushes
sniffs the ground
raises one leg
waters the
dark knight hybrid tea rose stems
ignores a red fire hydrant

they continue
to the convenience store
he buys a newspaper for father
eventually to be
used by the dog
in the neighbor's house

later he brings
an already-read paper
next door,
rings the doorbell
as a shapely mrs dowd opens it
she wears a white fluffy bathrobe
with a loosely tied bow

he hears mr dowd call
from upstairs, and
the dog runs inside;
when the door closes
he glances through
a lightly frosted glass door

mrs dowd turns to go upstairs
drops her robe on the floor
as she grasps the banister
before climbing
polished wood steps

gives the young boy,
for a fleeting moment,
a *folies bergère* show
he will remember forever

cheeseburger

stopped at a fast-food place
fresh burgers, hot fries
add the cheese and diet soda
a meal fit for a corpulent president

take a seat in the rear
next to a large glass window
see cars and trucks fly past —
my drink has too many cubes

i notice two men walk in
their hoodies cover hidden faces
quickly, a cash register opens
a day's receipts handed over

they run out — police run in
silent alarms pressed
as i chew a bite of burger, i notice
handcuffs flashed, quickly adjusted

not a bad lunch on a mild sunny day
food, a show, and crime don't pay

doctor   doctor

the patient is terminal
we all are   eventually
everything and everyone dies

if we take care of ourselves
life might be longer
or easier

yet we debase our bodies
while the civilized world
coughs pollutants into the air

the sun now bakes the earth
as the atmosphere atrophies
and the world starts a death rattle

glaciers melt   seas overflow
ocean currents change course
and the leader of a mighty nation

hurls ketchup and profanities at walls
ignores science's warnings
of impending doom

don't call the doctor again
call the undertaker
reserve some plots at a cemetery

drones in new york

they claim to see them
fifteen feet across
they fly over homes
they fly over malls
i hear many people in supermarkets
drone on about drones
what if they are aliens
small   green   tiny
looking for a hot meal
do we offer them chicken soup
or vegan green pea soup

i'm sure there are lonely people
looking for new relationships
maybe they'll buy the teeny visitors a florida condo
bring them to a warm, sunny, low-tax state

where republicans will gather them,
place them in a bus, then send them back north
            to freeze
since they have no clothes and the federal
government
sent their spaceship drones to nevada's area 51

now stranded in liberal manhattan,
probably times square,
where nobody will notice they are different
but part of the crowds —
city politicians register them to vote
eventually, their child can be a president
like one whose mother was an illegal alien

black pearl

japanese hanadama
top grade pearls
exceptional, expensive, nice
lustrously strung thrice
grace her tall, thin neck

across a room on a couture
paris made dress
with a low-cut blouse
from famous fashion house
the model, a twig of a girl

the only one
a human black pearl
in a caucasian sea
her hourly fees high
as suitors line up

their intentions nigh
clothes are what drives
men's urges high
to tease a little and
flash some silky skin

only right words can win the sin
and leave the fabrics
on the floor —
except for pearls
now naked and demure

be the tornado

gather your winds
unleash the fury within
don't hold back
let the world know you
face the ignoble
ignore the ignorable

lemons of society
sour happiness
blow past the passable
rule your life to its fullest
enjoy a sweet, succulent
watermelon of life

devour the tasty fruits of living
and know deep down in your heart
when the angel of death visits
you will ride the wind
with your chin up
         without regret

just another school shooting

as a twelve-year-old
        my garage was a fort
the large wooden double doors swung shut
locked, the drawbridge sealed tight
        i was protected
        the world's bullies can't touch me

today, two people died at school
their safe place breached
        a young child and substitute teacher
        the drawbridge was down
a secure place of learning
exposed to a deadly gun's plunder

how many forts need to be taken
and coffins buried
        before gun-loving politicians
        stop stuffing bank accounts
        with blood-soaked gun lobby cash
        obviously
thoughts and prayers
            don't protect innocents
because there
        was just another school
shooting
    today

breakup

they held hands
fingers intertwined
under a heartbreak moon

as she slices his heart open
bleeding salty tears
her sweet cherry pie words
drip with syrupy sugar

their love ends
he is monogamous
and she needs
an open arrangement

because magnets
don't always attract
all the time

full circle

the universe is immense
too many stars
not enough fingers and toes
yet coincidence happens
    without looking
an obituary in the local paper
shows an old lady's picture
gray hair   facial creases   name bolded

below the obit is her maiden name
i flash back
  fifty years back
she sixteen
    i seventeen
teenagers from different pasts, faiths, skin colors
clothes scattered about   our body's entwined

one summer
love hotter than the sun
but cold of winter froze things
plus
she lived in a different state
and i was too young to drive

urban farmette

when guests enter my home
they're surprised in my dining room
standing in the middle,
on the table, is my chicken

a multicolored metal rooster
awaits the platters
as my dining guests do, too
i assure them

their food is safe
let's eat and not worry
roosters don't lay eggs
nor does the tall tin pink flamingo

standing aloof
in my family room

eyes of love

she has them
both alluring and irresistible
falling in love is easy
those brown orbs
have a way of signaling
without words
intentions
yet i know
what they say
what they want
and somehow

what she desires

i don't have answers

a swarm of humanity
buzzes across borders
cities overwhelmed
    where to put them
how to care for them

for most:
it's a journey of survival
to live
    with a full belly
to live
    without drug gangs
to live
    in safety

many want a wall
many want to jail them
many want to send them back
to hunger, danger, death
when all they want
    is to live

one life at a time

christmas eve

holy night   all is bright
not all is right
as snowflakes fall
pews are full
they sing joyful prayers
to an innocent manger baby doll

the congregation rejoices
a family sits together in front
and directly behind them is
their lustful divorced neighbor
     who inhales
the husband's cologne
as it wafts off her skin
from a dalliance hours earlier

while choir hymns resonate
a celibate celebrates rebirth
in more ways than religious

divorcee thinks of remarriage
with someone else's husband
while priest fights desires
due to his consoling her
and her effusive gratefulness
with home shades drawn
mid-afternoons in gray sky december

joy to the world
santa's elves gleefully sing
a divorced lustful woman
might soon get   a sinful ring

fish eyes

the market has them on ice
rigid, frozen,
blank stares
see them peer at me
similar to deer in headlights
or some dates i've been on
when you ask
a simple get-to-know-you question
and they look at you
trying to come up with an answer
and that night
you end up in bed
with a breathing
motionless,
intellectually dead fish

jolly old london

the twits tumble along
twirl their temptations
while walking, or stumbling
on manchester street

they try to attract lovelies
to buy them a fun time
of drinks and dinner
as the evening runs along

their moggy's trimmed
eager to please
low-cut tops out to tease
underskirt, commando rules

bad boys roam all night
some get into a fight
as twitettes dance hours long
and sing sweetly to a swifty song

morning after they gather up
their shoes, clothes and say goodbye
leave a place they've never been
with a kiss and memories of carnal sin

early morning drama

breakfast is usually calm
pour a glass of milk
take six chocolate cookies
start to dunk
one at a time
while i watch the news
on my phone

look out the kitchen window
see a grey squirrel
with a bushy, bushy tail
scoot across the street
between speeding cars

half-way across
it turns around
scoots back to the curb
it didn't look both ways
before crossing
      s p l a t
      flat
couldn't help but see that

still had three cookies left
poured more milk
dunked one at a time

resurrection

boring
    the marriage is boring
same old, same old
    something needs to change
they decide to open it
    serial monogamy with permission
ground rules set
    both agree
after months of dates
    each found an *other*
and settled in a routine
    same old, same old
boring
    decide to close the marriage
and start over
    begin again *together*
resurrecting
    a monogamous marriage

reality of life

illness and death go together
like smiles and laughs bond
how do you deal with a pet's demise

my maltese named farley went blind
at fifteen years he developed cataracts
shook from nerves and refused to walk

when the veterinarian made the decision
we were devastated
now i'm aware of family and friends

who become ill with terrible outcomes
modern medicine prolongs a life
but eventually, the breakdown happens

nobody wants to talk openly
it festers in our minds and disrupts sleep
unable to acknowledge   the inevitable

heart flutters

it's early evening,
randomly, i met her
a few months ago,
now, she's boarding the train
with a one-way ticket
to deep in my heart,
when i finally decide
to leave my old baggage
on the station platform
and begin over
with a fresh start
to go to
where i always wanted

with no return ticket

Brian Sicknick

the january sixth insurrection
rampaged through the capital
defiling flags, halls, and congress

a uniformed police officer died
because of the battering he took
trying to defend congress

his name will be read
in our history books
along with nathan hale

and other heroes who served
with heroism and honor
who made the ultimate sacrifice

may-december

there was a young lady from nantucket
whose elderly husband kicked the bucket
thought he still had some youthful stamina
yet had trouble with a drooping banana
rest in peace, the preacher did preach
as his teen widow rested on a beach
his wealth and accumulated money
now spent by his young honey-bunny
the moral of this little poetic tale
is look for an elderly wealthy male

food for thought

saw sexy sally shop for food
her cart filled with lots of treats
surprised, since she sells tasty eats
privately, as a sugar baby online
many old men think she's fine
buying her fine food and wine,
jewels, cars, and almost anything
but none stepped up with a diamond ring
everyone knows she's a fine fling
finally, her cart slowly rolls past me
her blouse unbuttoned for all to see
what bought her a brand new red ferrari

honesty

today is the present
the sun is out
sky clear
wind gusts gently caress my cheeks

in the past
i had flown with eagles
and made friends
with the lowly worms underground
when i mentally visited both

today is the present
i'm okay
some friends have no more pain
it ended for them when they ended
yet i'm still here to remember them
they will live forever with me
today, i'm okay

riding through manhattan

the cab driver is foreign,
speaks to me a little
i don't understand his english
when we go around union square
two women stand on the corner
garish   hard looking   working girls
noontime specials, i guess
tough times
my driver opens his window
waves   calls out
they must know him
wave back with one finger
i smile at them

on park benches
raggedy men sleep
unshaved   disheveled
cops walk past
trash cans overflow onto sidewalks
broken needles litter the street
traffic packed tight
red lights frustrate
people walk between cars
we continue downtown
s l o w l y
my date waits in my hotel room
no rush
both fully paid for

her rat city

streets littered with throwaways
paper, food, candy, and
people
edibles taken away
not by sanitation workers
but unpaid aides who scurry about
trying to avoid working people
when they leave their dens
in the dark crevices of the city
to find food flung and discarded
by rat-fearing eaters
that decry rodents
who stroll streets searching
to sustain themselves

finally, one day she had enough
told the low-life moocher to leave

never see me again

returned his cheap-ass
fake diamond ring

five senses

she is a vision to behold
beautiful beyond expectations
my senses erupt in anticipation

my tongue glides over soft, smooth skin
the gustation of my taste glands arouses
suppressed feelings

pheromones
an olfactory explosion
i cannot get enough of her perfume

when my ears receive the audition
i love you i cannot decide which sense
is the most valuable

the tactician of my hand on her
secreted body parts unseen in daylight
completes my sensory time with her

august 31st

the summer season ends there
hot love in warm weather now a memory
lovers kiss goodbye till next year
winter chills romance in many ways
especially
when you have cold,
snow-filled, dark days

smiles and giggles turn to gloom
sunny rays await your next love
take a ticket
take a turn
ex-lovers move on
there'll be new conquests
new *forevers* to love
till the next summer season ends

tears for democracy

money has more value than oaths
what benefits few cost the many more
constitutional government skewered
the rule of law bent by corruptibles
by a functionally illiterate cult leader
who enriches family, friends, followers
as bigotry and racism rears its hungry head
while the "others" suffer indignities
while promised falsehoods of prosperity

missing

a grandson is missing
he hasn't seen him in months
no milk carton picture yet
he isn't lost or kidnapped
yet still missing

his daughter is separated
they live an hour away
rarely is he seen
except for seven days in summer
when a place rented at the beach
    then he stays with them

if called, he only answers yes or no
won't expand his conversation
a quiet kid, a playstation pro at fourteen
his grandson's missing from his life

library pickup

as i stand in the middle of the library
surrounded by row after row of books
staid, somber, quiet

> *deathly quiet*

a few people sit and read
at tables scattered about
they don't understand
the secrets in this space

many titles to pick from
a lifetime of learning
on page after page
i'll pick one from a shelf
then sit in a nook
           by myself
           by myself
              reading

five

i know where i come from
my roots go back to latvia
to the old country
at least five generations

dna goes back further
all the way to the holy city of medina
seems i am related to the holy prophet
whose faith is housed there

the test traced my ancestors to spain,
eastern europe, and israel
where i have the markers of priesthood
a direct descendant of moses' brother aaron

with all the holiness in my blood
i am not blinded by religious doctrine
while congregations read their books
of prayers written for them

i sit in my backyard
            contemplating life, death
and the vastness of the universe

at seventeen

i once owned a casino
and suckers i'd slay
i'd gamble for a pot
almost all-day

never lost a lot
in any way
poetry isn't
my only talent, i'd say

until my mother
with a frown
closed me down

poetry is power

freedom is in the words i write
not in laws passed by politicians

poets have free rein to explore
to hate and love a lot more

than most folks who live blandly
or a beautiful starlet with burly security

untouchable even if i did try
those men would surely see i die

but in stanzas, she adores my body
fights with others to beget my baby

our love plays all night and day
as i leave her bed, she begs me -*stay*

but i close the door on glorious intimacy
in a final loving couplet with delicacy

smile

she's divorced
bleached bottle-blond
waist-length, long hair
bright white smile
shapely at forty
with a small, potty belly
her online fan page
earns a million a year
where it shows nude videos
of her doing things
with her breasts, nipples
plus various devices,
some electrified,
many would consider
obscene and pornographic
yet viewers continue to pay
to watch her explicit movies
unaware
her adult twenty-something son
is the cameraman
smile

recipe for cake

take out
    five-quart kitchen food mixer
    box of all-purpose flour
    salt
    butter bars
    chocolate pieces to melt
    yeast packet
    bowl
    icing
    baking pan
    silicon scraper
then
check wallet
credit cards
car keys
drive to the bakery
purchase is much easier
drive home
take out ice-cold milk
eat delicious chocolate cake just bought

put everything away till more ambitious

relationship

mothers and daughters
have a special bond

usually

it crosses
most boundaries of
propriety
where secrets
told in confidence
are kept

sincere advice given
is not always taken
or even acted upon
which is different
than a mom's links
with a son
who is naturally
born to run

inspiration

poetry is a muse
irresistible and
alluring

poems come in many
different shapes
and formats
    some tall
    some short
many don't know when to stop as they have no
punctuation
but use meter   word flow   space
to guide the reader

satisfyingly attractive
to write and read
yet don't expect coins
to be thrown at you
unless the poem really sucks

lost love

we had a solid love
never out of sight
always in my heart
she was my bright light

years together
we thought forever
but true love is hard
never thought i'd let go

kids need food and baths
don't know how i'll manage
i didn't really want to leave
to go home without her

today was a tough one
tears and heart-break broke me
i really did try to be brave
had a hard time at her grave

joan 1953

eight years old
third grade
he transferred to a new school
in october after school began
most seats taken
seated way in the back
in an empty seat
next to a pretty blond girl
always wore a skirt

teacher was elderly
sat in front on a wooden stool
never walked the room

he asked the girl to show her undies
slowly his hand slid up her leg
she seemed to enjoy it
this went on for months

when summer came
promotions arrived
eventually went to different schools
they never spoke again —
seventy-two years later
he still remembers her

manhattan streets

a lot of strange people walk the streets
papaya king's gone along with their eats
beggars go hungry, a dollar's not enough
life in manhattan is pretty tough

a hooker's a whore who'll go in any door
every john to them is another don juan
love's a commodity without any security
to her cash talks, and nobody walks

street gangs roam with knives of chrome
stick a bitch if she should snitch
they rob and pillage north of the village
but south of harlem, gangs rule the turf

trepidation and fear are rampant each year
police are feckless; citizens helpless
throw'em in jail, don't give'em bail
only safe at home; don't go out to roam

where lots of weird people
walk the city's streets

searching

broken hearts
are cast aside
as lovers watch
reluctantly
from the sidelines
while they wait
for a winner
to swipe right
then knock on their door

not realizing
if selected
they are the prize

small losses

when lovers part
hearts torn asunder
their worlds stop turning
white clouds turn dark gray

some say *so long sucker*
move to someone new
to them, it's no big deal
it was infatuation– not true

when depression grinds its teeth
and a river of tears waterfalls down
it's a big deal trying to heal
even heartless people start to kneel

they pray for answers as to why
and many feel they will suddenly die
but the answer is not an easy one
i say screw the sobbing, it's their loss

loss

everyone will have it
we need to deal
as best we can in life

can't be deterred every time
yet many losses can be avoided
like a walk on broken glass

we see it scattered on the street
but sometimes can't avoid it
and crush down with bleeding feet

but the unhinged among us
are allowed to buy
military-style guns without checks

dead children in schools result
responsible politicians have a response
they offer meaningless thoughts and prayers

until their loved ones are shot and buried
no meaningful laws will be enacted,
at that time, they will grieve in reality

mister right now

after her divorce
moved away
far away
to start over
finish school
work long hours
socially settled and selective
for immediate satisfaction
not long-term love
desire for traditional
white picket fence —
been there   done that
now, libido freed
life explodes
opportunities
live in the moment

supermarket parking lot

he had to run in
buy a few things
the chocolate croissants
small chunks of dark sweetness
oozes from ends
spoke to him
lined up on a shelf
freshly baked
still warm
sell control yields
salivary desire rules
a plastic bag
opened
filled
paid
eaten in the car
while he watches
a parade of thin young women
park and walk in the market
wearing skin-tight leggings —
at eighty years old
only pastries are orgasmic

whose side is god on in war

the good side or the devils
when mothers, children, fathers
are bombed to cellular levels
and shreds of humanity are lost
in rubble of civilization

whose side is god on in war
women raped,
killed, bodies mutilated
innocents lose limbs in youth
parents blinded, bodies decay
strewn about, only the odor
of rotting civilians
gives their location

whose side is god on in war
when religious leaders
on both sides
pray for success in battle
they ask the almighty
to slay the enemy,
to vanquish them completely
not sparing even one individual

perhaps the answer is simply
humans are extremely brutal,
and god, if in existence,
does not care

loner

a friendless child
no one to play with
no kids on the block
after school goes home
does math and reading
never outside playing football
from
sewer cover to sewer cover
with neighborhood children
not because of an infirmity
but it's a problem
when
you live on a cul-de-sac
with only one sewer

observer

on the top floor of a walk up
in a leased flat with three actors
he sits by his window with pad and pen
the only writer of the bunch

below, eighth street greenwich village
hums with commerce as street vendors
offer illicit drugs to willing buyers
who force unwilling young women
into working the streets for their drugs

he sees things others ignore
ink starts to flow word after word
his novel builds line after line
each page full of observed details

newspapers reported on police
who take cash from vicious pimps, shakedown
deadly drug dealers, then bury dirty cash in
backyards under grandmother's red rosebushes

brown dirt from a cop's brooklyn home
is the bank for his greenbacks
until needed for vacations far away
and jewelry for a hidden mistress

while a wife works long retail hours
and children attend expensive private schools
where nuns teach religion and ethics
and his home rings of an upright family

mother acorn

lies on her side
stem firm
cap mottled
seeds unberthed
waits for moisture
to soften its shell,
release offspring
under protective shade
of a mighty oak tree
to begin anew life's cycle

pain

if i were to be cut
the incision would hurt
pain is felt
all animals feel discomfort
but do all living things feel it

trees are known
to communicate
when drought or fire
encroach upon them

vegetables are plucked
washed
sliced
sometimes diced
do they not feel pain

are we not smart enough to
to speak their language
does broccoli live pain-free
although it pains me
to smell it cook
or eaten

tea sandwiches

high tea is a tradition
dainty porcelain cups
floral designs
set on tiny plates
pinky out when lifted
with small crustless
cucumber and cream cheese
bite-sized temptations
which leave men
real men
hungry
wanting a pint or two
with thick
piled high meats
stuffed between
sliced bread with chewy crusts
and a bountiful waitress
who brings cheer and glee
on an otherwise typical day

city living

can you live in a city
while remaining a country kid

can black asphalt replace
the dark coal mines of youth
when rail cars moved north
and pieces fell off to heat our home

can bluegrass sung by granny
and uncle jedediah, on his fiddle
be replaced by rock'n roll and soul
while i look up and can't see any clouds

as city smog and pollution hide the sun
which warms cold forest creeks
where we bare-ass swam on hot july days
then dry off on a blanket tightly enwrapped

gently rolling treed hills are a memory
replaced by skyscrapers of steel and glass
i won't die here   health care's better than
back home, where the doctor came twice a year

but given a choice of where to rest forever
bury me in the green glen back home
birds can sing to me, children run barefoot
over my final bed

stuff

what do you do
when a loved one dies
with their possessions
accumulated in a lifetime

the choice becomes
keep it all
or throw everything away

except

their things are markers
of how they lived
a memorial of
their humor, interests, loves,
the boxes of papers, pictures, photos
are to be kept until you, too, are gone,
then someone
who doesn't know
will dump it all,
unceremoniously,
in the bin;
then death becomes real,
you become forgotten,
everything   becomes   stuff

fox hunting

from my rear window
i see dozens of canada geese
land on a snowcapped lawn
to squark and strut aimlessly
impervious to arctic cold winds —
from the far side of the field, by bushes,
a red fox slithers forward
his potential lunch unaware
slowly   slowly   slowly   he crawls
then an *explosion of speed forward*
      wings flap   frantically hover
          birds fly
   gray feathers   float in air
the predator jumps up   snaps at the flock
    missing his meal
my eighty-year-old next-door neighbor died
his widow of a year is still youngish
with a working libido
she looks out her window at me,
watching the birds,
waves to come over,
it's lunchtime —
she wears a sheer blouse
with no bottoms
maybe
i'll have better luck than the fox
i think i know what she's serving to eat

bronx metaphors

the roosters are not yet awake
while hunts point wholesale market
in the bronx hums when produce arrives
trucks load/unload
    buyers come early
    sellers anxiously wait
face to face
    offers to sell
    offers to buy
deals made
money trades hands
inside
    cash only
outside
    cash only
in the darkness
of the bronx streets
are sexy nouns
looking for quick deals
while cars filled with men
pick up metaphors
not realizing
they are not what they seem

soon disappointed
by the preposition
to their proposition
they discover they have
a dangling participle
left hanging

unnamed woman

taste my tongue
the lady implores her neighbor
when she lies down next to him
while he works to fix a cabinet
in her carpeted living room —
he senses intimacy is imminent
her expression explodes
with desire
starts an affair —
her husband fails in marital duties
leaves her frustrated with a high libido
to search wherever
includes friends of either gender
until she finally finds
a single lover
who agrees to marry her
      then a divorce

her new husband
leaves the beehive
to go to work
the queen bee's
worker drones
buzz about the house
to work on things
        including her

mirage

while i sit at my desk
a black cat scampers away
like a hurricane's wind, i
thought i saw it
pass the door

seen today
here no more
field mice scatter about
when they hear
a black cat roar

loving husband

in poker
a facial expression
is a tell
if a good hand is in the cards
or not
a husband of twenty years
who sleeps with a sex worker
shortly after his wife gives birth
can expect a near-miss kiss
when he tries a lip lock
on his inauguration day
and she turns her head away
is a tell about a marriage

they said to me

your poem today is different
from other works you wrote

how do i tell them the truth
it wasn't written purposely that way

i had to wait for my muse
to whisper words in my ear

all i did was write them down

the end

For more of
elliot m rubin's books
www.CreativeFiction.net

follow him on
Instagram

elliot_m_rubin
people poems

www.ingramcontent.com/pod-product-compliance
Lightning Source LLC
Chambersburg PA
CBHW070703100426
42735CB00039B/2683